What's it like to be a...
CHEF

Written by Susan Cornell Poskanzer
Illustrated by Karen E. Pellaton

Troll Associates

Special Consultant: Anthony Molfetas, *Seven Seas Restaurant, Ramsey, New Jersey.*

Library of Congress Cataloging-in-Publication Data

Poskanzer, Susan Cornell.
    What's it like to be a chef / by Susan Cornell Poskanzer;
illustrated by Karen E. Pellaton.
        p.   cm.—(Young careers)
    Summary: Describes the work of a chef as he goes about his job of
cooking a variety of meals in a big restaurant.
    ISBN 0-8167-1797-4 (lib. bdg.)   ISBN 0-8167-1798-2 (pbk.)
    1. Cooks—Juvenile literature.   [1. Cooks.   2. Occupations.]
I. Pellaton, Karen E., ill.   II. Title.   III. Series.
TX652.5.P67   1990
641.5'7'023—dc20   89-34390

JJ 641.5

What's it like to be a...
CHEF

Hi, my name is Casey. Today I came to work with my Uncle Peppi. He's a chef in a big restaurant. I've seen him cook at home many times. But today is special. So, I'm visiting him at the restaurant.

Meet Uncle Peppi. He's wearing what chefs have worn for a long time. I like his tall hat. He is wearing his white jacket, tie, and apron.

Whisk

Mixing Bowl

Baking Sheet

"Good morning," he says to the bakers.
The bakers started working at three-thirty
this morning. Their kitchen is filled with the
sweet smell of bread and cakes baking in huge
ovens. The chief baker is Bruno. He gives me a
warm roll.

In the pantry my uncle meets Bob, the steward. Bob orders all the food for the restaurant. About one hundred people will eat lunch here today. Bob orders a lot of food.

Pantry
Shelves

Eggplants

Scale

Bob checks arriving food to make sure it is fresh. He weighs it to make sure he gets the right amounts.

Back in the kitchen I smell spicy sauces
cooking. I hear soups bubbling. My face feels
warm near the big open pots.

I see Uncle Peppi's helpers getting food ready. Some are cutting bright red and yellow peppers. Others are cleaning smooth white mushrooms. Some are peeling golden yellow apples.

My uncle looks at today's menu.

"How do you know what to cook?" I ask.

"Good chefs are artists," answers Peppi. "They use their imagination. They think about foods that will look and taste good together. Sometimes I think up new ideas, or I find them in cookbooks. Then I try them. If they're good, I add them to my menu."

"Are you ready to help?" asks Uncle Peppi.

"Could I?" I ask. "I'm an artist, too. I once invented the peanut butter and sardine sandwich."

My uncle laughs. "Well then, you *can* help me," he says.

I follow Uncle Peppi into a walk-in box.
A walk-in box is a restaurant refrigerator.
It's so big we can walk right into it. It's like a
cold closet with lots of food. Uncle Peppi has
many walk-in boxes. One is for fish. One is for
meat. One is for vegetables. Another is for milk,
cheese, and eggs.

Uncle Peppi hands me two boxes of eggs.
He carries a bowl of cheese and some peeled
onions. I walk *very* carefully to his work table.

Pepper Mill

"When I was young," he says, "I worked in
many kitchens. I watched many chefs. I was an
apprentice. I helped and I learned. We have three
apprentices here now. Watch that one. She'll be a
great chef one day."

19

Waiters begin to call out lunch orders.
Everyone listens.

Suddenly, everyone is busy. People move quickly to cook the orders. The kitchen gets hotter. The warm smells of onions, herbs, and spices fill the air.

Uncle Peppi hears an order for a soufflé. A soufflé is made of whipped eggs. It puffs up when it cooks in the oven.

Uncle Peppi puts onions into a pan of hot oil. He flips the onions up into the air. I wonder how he catches them over and over.

He drops in a pinch of salt. Some of the salt
hits the flame of the stove. It flickers like a
hundred little firecrackers.

"Time for you," says Uncle Peppi. "I need eight eggs in this bowl."

Slowly, I break the shells against the bowl. I want to show Uncle Peppi that I can cook, too. I don't want any eggshells to fall into the bowl.

Uncle Peppi's eyes sparkle as he looks into
the bowl. "No shells! Good job, Casey," he says
as he whips the eggs with a wire whisk.

He adds the onions, cheese, and other things.
Peppi smiles as he pours the mixture into tall
pans. He slides the pans into the oven.

Next Uncle Peppi quickly walks through the kitchen. He wants to make sure everything is running smoothly. He works hard. He stirs a stew. He arranges food. It looks beautiful on the warmed plates.

He grates whole nutmeg spice into a sauce.
Some nutmeg drops on the floor. In a wink, a
helper mops the floor clean.

After a while, Uncle Peppi says, "It's time.
It's your special day, Casey. Follow Frank."

I walk behind the waiter. We go through
swinging kitchen doors out into the restaurant.
The tables are filled with people. They are talking
and eating Uncle Peppi's wonderful food.

I sit very tall. I put my napkin on my lap.
I feel very grown-up. Soon Uncle Peppi walks
through the swinging doors. He carries a big
tray. He puts three dishes on the table and sits
down with me.

"Happy birthday, Casey!" says Uncle Peppi.

Uncle Peppi has made a special birthday
lunch just for me. Peppi is not just a wonderful
chef. He's a wonderful uncle, too!